YOUR KNOWLEDGE HAS VALUE

Cristiano Mendez

Advanced CAD/CAM Systems

GRIN Verlag

Bibliografische Information der Deutschen Nationalbibliothek:

Die Deutsche Bibliothek verzeichnet diese Publikation in der Deutschen National-
bibliografie; detaillierte bibliografische Daten sind im Internet über http://dnb.d-
nb.de/ abrufbar.

Imprint:

Copyright © 2013 GRIN Verlag GmbH
Druck und Bindung: Books on Demand GmbH, Norderstedt Germany
ISBN: 978-3-656-62476-9

This book at GRIN:

http://www.grin.com/en/e-book/270846/advanced-cad-cam-systems

GRIN - Your knowledge has value

Der GRIN Verlag publiziert seit 1998 wissenschaftliche Arbeiten von Studenten, Hochschullehrern und anderen Akademikern als eBook und gedrucktes Buch. Die Verlagswebsite www.grin.com ist die ideale Plattform zur Veröffentlichung von Hausarbeiten, Abschlussarbeiten, wissenschaftlichen Aufsätzen, Dissertationen und Fachbüchern.

Visit us on the internet:

http://www.grin.com/

http://www.facebook.com/grincom

http://www.twitter.com/grin_com

2013

[Advanced CAD/CAM]

Advanced CAD/CAM

Contents

CAD/CAM systems in production of tooling and dies:

CAD/CAM is the advanced technology used in manufacturing process by the assistance of computers and software's. In traditional manufacturing drawing is done by drafting in which modification and prototyping took more time and cost, but the latest CAD software's eliminated this by software interface like ProE. Not only designing but also manufacturing was hectic involving lot of machine for single operations but latest advanced CNC machines integrated with computer known as CAM avoids these troubles (Jassi, n.d.).

Integrated CAD/CAM Systems:

The latest advancement in the CAD/CAM systems is the integrated CAD/CAM systems. This integrated system has been classified into two types as CAD-centric and CAM-centric according to where it is used. In CAD-centric the CAD system interface is the mainly used one but it also has the CAM features to support. For ex, solid works which is CAD software have this CAM integration in its interface provided by Delcam. Likewise the CAM-centric is the one mainly interfaced for NC programming but it has integration with CAD to make it easier to modify the 3D model within them. For ex, Cimatron provides built in CAD interface to make geometrical corrections. Thus these integrations provide lots of advantages but full features of both CAD and CAM hasn't been brought together (**Yares, 2012**)

But Min Hou in his article about the integration mentions that because of this integration a better communication has been formed between both the systems which made production easier. He says that without the integration the part produced in CAD should be recreated in the CAM for generating the tool path and programs which is eliminated by the integration. It reduced the design cost also opened platform for new researches. The integration helps to import 3D model created by the CAD into the CAM as wireframe or even surface so that tool paths can be generated for them to manufacture by CNC (Hou, 2012)

Die Development:

Development of progressive dies was been always a trouble with conventional machining because of the error and its expensive also lots of time is wasted in the redesigning. This kind of problems in design and manufacturing is solved by the advancement in the CAD CAM system made by Gerber systems technology (publication, 1984). Gaston Pelletier an engineer at CSSC says that before few years if there is a need to create very less tolerance parts in manufacturing

3

then it became a bottle neck process at the CAD area. It has been taken days or even weeks to deliver the design to the manufacturing. But by the AutoGraph system by the Gerber systems eliminated these problems. The die layout is easily created by this and the assembly can be easily exploded. And the features like clearance, scrap, dowel holes can be easily positioned. The cross sectional view of entire tool assembly can be easily displayed. Similar components can be easily recreated and modifies by just changing the parameters and the system automatically regenerates new model for it (Anon., 1984)

Parallel processing in tooling:

The emerged advancement in cutting edge tool in order to improve its efficiency is parallel processing. It is nothing but speeding up the processing of NC programs by making several processes running in the background. In previous days it was done with the help of multiple processors but now it is been carried out by the software, we can simultaneously work on the new drawing while the system generates tool path for the old one **(Anon., 2009)**.

Computer Aided Process Planning:

It is planning of a process with the aid of the computer. Process planning in manufacturing is nothing but the formation of the route sheets and organizing the sequence of operations and allotting the work centers for particular operation to produce products. The firms needed this operation to be done by automated way because the manual process planning consist of disadvantages like

- Depends on person's experience
- Time consuming
- Changes can't be made easier

It is good to integrate the CAPP with the CAD and CAM system for good benefits. There are two types of CAPP approach which are Retrieval CAPP and Generative CAPP. In retrieval the plan is stored for a part and for a new similar part the plan is derived from modifying the older one but alternatively in generative one the plan is generated from the beginning (Pandey, n.d.)

Integrating CAPP and CAD/CAM:

Between the designing and manufacturing the bridge is the process planning. It is the process of selecting tools to be used, the best manufacturing method and its sequence. The CAPP does this work automatically and more efficiently. The two types of information required

4

communicating between the CAPP and CAD CAM is the geometrical data (the part's design) and the technological data (method for manufacturing the part), (Jung Hyun Han, 2001). **Feature technology** is the latest advancement to provide this integration because it interprets the features to develop the manufacturing sequence. After a lot of research in this area, Khoshnevis develops Intelligent incremental process planning which has a knowledge based approach for identifying the feature and for the selection of process space search algorithm is being used (H. B. Marri, 1998).

The feature based machining sequence is also done by taking account of the tool capabilities and optimized according to the process and the cost. A setup is generated and optimal sequence is found for each step. It uses Standard for Exchange for Product Model Data (STEP) for input and output so it can be ported to CAD systems (Jung Hyun Han, 2001). Although there is many research for the link between the CAPP and the CAD systems there is nothing much upon CAPP integration with the CAM systems. The STEP based tool path generation for the machining of planar surfaces which is a rough machining has features like data extraction and volume slicing module also NC code automatic generator and CL file generation module. So this STEP file with these modules easily identifies the internal and external features of the part and helps in generating the tool path very easily (M. Liang, 1996)

(Huikang K. Miao, 2002) Manufacturing has become easier by the feature based automatic process planning. He says that CAPP is achieved automatically by its features and automatically the tool path is started to generate and exported by I-IDEAS. Taxonomy with 3-axis feature has been defined including inner profile blind hole and outer profile etc., as shown below.

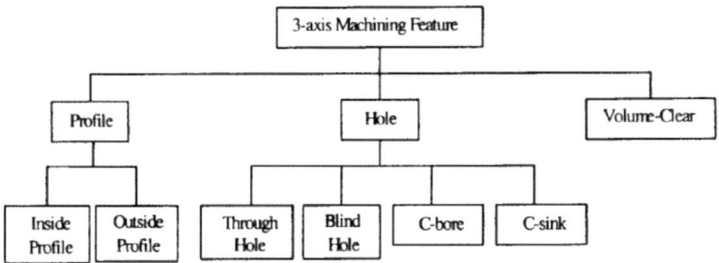

Feature technology in CAD/CAPP/CAM:

Feature-based design:

When a product model is built-up by a set of design features then it is known as feature based design. For a designer it will be easier to have more pre-defined shapes but it will increase the size of pre-defined library, so the one advantage of this is we can edit the existing library by simply adding deleting and modifying the existing features (Chen, 1995). In designing and manufacturing the adding and removing of materials is not same always and the design features can't be used in the manufacturing directly

For example let's look at the following picture

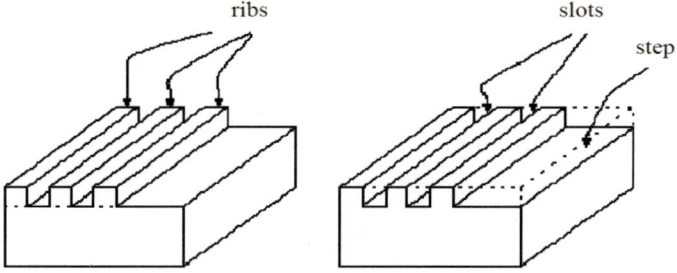

Source: Chen, 1995

In this design the designer would have designed it as ribs while creating this model as we see in first part, but when it goes for manufacturing it is seen by him as the slot and steps that must be removed from the stock material. One way to remove this trouble is to use the manufacturing method in the designing but it will reduce the flexibility of the designer and their freedom (Salomons, 1995). Also for this the designer has to look upon the manufacturing features from the earlier level of designing. So a solution developed for this is using two different features in designing and manufacturing and converting it into manufacturing features known as model conversion (Han, 2000)

Also the latest improvements in CAPP include:

- The design dimensions are translated to manufacturing automatically
- The tolerance are converted into manufacturing dimensions

- CAPP is made accessible for small and also medium scale industries

Rapid prototyping technologies:

Rapid prototyping is a technique used to produce parts or assembly using three dimensional data from the CAD. It creates the model layer by layer in an additive manner, and able to produce any complex shapes easily. It fabricates even plastic wood and thin sheets of metal. It has advantages like it gives higher speed in production and also flaws are easily detected and rectified (Patmullins, n.d.)

Stereolithography (sla):

It is the most widely used rapid prototyping technology. It builds the plastic parts by layer by layer by tracing the laser beam on the surface of a liquid polymer. The layer bonds to one another by self-adhesion. The recent advancement in this technology is integration of its molds with the injection molding process (Patmullins, n.d.) Among the different process the rapid plastic injection molding is more important. Stereolithography technique has higher speed and smooth finishing techniques. It has got a higher resolution as high as 60 μm (Decelles, 1996).

During these last year's lots of research has been carried out. Weiss have shown that this rapid prototype model can be used to get a shell of metal along with the help of epoxy resin which can be used for injection molding and metal forming (Weiss, 1990). Paul Jacobs has talked about the non-homogeneous property of SL models which is mechanical. He shown that these models are function of laser exposure and sooner knowledge about it will help to prevent the shrinkage which is formed during the part developing process (Jacobs, 1996). Likewise lot of research has been developed and demonstrated the performance of the SL technology so that it can be utilized for the injection molding process (Rahmati, 1997)

Fused deposition modeling:

It is second most widely used technology. A plastic filament is unwound from the coil and passed through the nozzle where it is heated and the material is made to flow over, by moving the nozzle accordingly the required geometry is formed accordingly. It can be used to create any shapes and features which is the primary advantage because of the additive feature. This technology is mostly used for rapid production of the new part. The models are also can be used the various tests and analysis like testing for the fluid flow and also various aerodynamic tests. Also there is an one more application in this area used for verification of the assembling procedures and also checking their properties like kinematical and dynamics. They also play

7

significant role in the medical field because of their advancements like forming prototypes for the bones. Because of the 3D prototype development it is very easier to view the model than the 2D drawing. Also the model can be easily tested by scaling down the testing forces, and the recreation, redesigning is made possible very easier. (GRIMM, 2004)

Works Cited

Anon., 1984. computer-aided design-computer-aided manufacturing. 1 Novenber.

Anon., 2009. Programming in parallel. *Manufacturing engineering*, October.

Chen, X.a.H.C.M., 1995. On editability of feature-based design. *Computer-Aided Design*, 27(December), pp.904-14.

Decelles, P.&.B.M., 1996. Direct AIM Prototype Tooling, 3D Systems. (November).

GRIMM, T.., 2004. User's Guide to Rapid Prototyping. *Society of Manufacturing Engineers*.

H. B. Marri, A.G.a.R.J.G., 1998. Computer-aided process a state of art. *The International Journal of Advanced Manufacturing Technology*, 14, pp.261-68.

Han, J.H..P.M.a.R.W.C., 2000. Manufacturing feature recognition from solid models. *IEEE Transactions on Robotics and Automation*, 16, pp.782-96.

Hou, M., 2012. *CAD/CAM Integration Based on Machining Features for Prismatic Parts*.

Huikang K. Miao, N.S.a.J.J.S., 2002. CAD-CAM integration using machining features. *Int. J. Computer Integrated Manufacturing*, 15, pp.296-318.

Jacobs, P.F., 1996. Recent Advances in Rapid Tooling from Stereolithography. *A Rapid Prototyping Conference*.

Jassi, N., n.d. *CAD / CAM fundamentals*. [Online] Available at: http://cadcamfunda.com/what_is_cadcam_ [Accessed 28 april 2013].

Jung Hyun Han, I.H.a.J.Y., 2001. Manufacturing feature recognition. *IEEE Transactions on Systems, Man*, 31(june), pp.373-80.

M. Liang, S.A.a.B.v.d.B., 1996. A STEP based tool path generation system for rough machining of planar surfaces. *Computers in Industry*, 32(December), pp.219-32.

Pandey, D.P.M., n.d. *Computer Aided Process*. [Online] Available at: http://paniit.iitd.ac.in/~pmpandey [Accessed 2013].

Patmullins, n.d. *RAPID PROTOTYPING*. [Online] Available at:
patmullins.com/img/RAPIDPROTOTYPINGCaseStudy.pps [Accessed 2013].

publication, N., 1984. *CAD-CAM builds die sets faster, easier.* [Online] Available at:
http://www.thefreelibrary.com/CAD-CAM+builds+die+sets+faster,+easier.-a03503413.

Rahmati, S.&.D., 1997. Stereolithography for Injection Mould tooling. *Rapid Prototyping Journal*, 3, pp.53-60.

Salomons, O.W., 1995. Computer Support in the Design of Mechanical Products:Constraint specification and satisfaction in feature based design formanufacturing. (June).

Weiss, 1990. A Rapid Tool Manufacturing System Based on Stereolithography and Thermal Spraying. *ASME Manufacturing Review*, 3, pp.40-48.

Yares, E., 2012. Do you really need integrated CAD/CAM? 1 August.